SLOW BUT DEADLY

WWII MEMOIRS
of an SBD Dive Bomber Pilot

Robert E. Anderson
Captain, United States Marine Corps
Served 1942-1946

WWII MEMOIRS

The author would like to thank the museums and other sources that kindly provided photographs for use in this book.

Printed and bound in the United States of America
First printing • ISBN # 978-1-930043-91-0
Copyright © 2011 Robert E. Anderson

All rights reserved. No part of this book may be reproduced, stored in a retrieval system, or transmitted in any form or by any means without permission from the author, except by a reviewer, who may quote briefly in a review.

To Order Additional Copies of this Book:
Please Call **1-800-628-0212**
$12.95 plus S&H

Scott Company Publishing
Kalispell, Montana
1-800-628-0212
scott@scottcompany.net

Foreword by Shirley Anderson

Three years ago, Bob "thought it would be fun" to write his WWII memoirs. Only a few copies were given to offspring who relished the stories of their Dad as a young man, who was sometimes prone to error. However, as those living WWII combat vets are dying at the rate of 1,000 a day, the interest in anecdotal writings of that period of time seems to have broadened. Thus <u>Slow But Deadly</u> was published, an edited copy with related pictures.

In Bob's introduction to his memoirs, he stated, "I wish my Dad had done the same." If indeed, wisdom comes with age, perhaps it is because the elderly have been privileged to be close to several generations. For the two of us, it has been four generations; our parents in the early part of the century, the two of us a part of the WWII era living the resultant changes in society, our three children who were teens and young adults during the turbulent 60s and 70s, and finally our grandchildren whose global outlook enables them to travel from country to country as easily as we went from state to state.

How I would like to read memoirs from the younger generations. Perhaps "times are different now" could be replaced by a real effort to understand the challenges faced by each generation. What's wrong? What's right? What is good and worth preserving? What changes are needed in our thinking?

So, whether you are an early airplane buff, WWII history scholar, want to understand the era, curious about the "greatest generation", or just want a little adventure, enjoy this small slice of history.

*1947 Post WWII
Glacier Park R&R*

*Bob & Shirley Anderson
1948 - 1998
50th Wedding Anniversary*

Dedication

This book is dedicated to those pilots whose experiences paralleled those of the author, but whose luck ran out and denied them the pleasures of relating their stories to others.

Jake Perrin, R&R

Jake Perrin

11-1-1943 Andy and McSpad

McCruden "McSpad"

Sam LaRue and gunner

Sam LaRue

Bob McEvoy, brother-in-law, stateside 1946, well fed and happy

Introduction

Why it is that as one grows older there appears to be a memory spurt reminding one of happenings long past, I do not know. However, in that it is true, and family members have suggested that some stories relating to WWII should be recorded, these following anecdotal bits and pieces are now being put on a computer hard drive. Although it doesn't seem that much of this would be of interest to others, I wish my Dad had done the same. That being said, here goes...

Being born 11/28/22 was a real stroke of luck. That made me the perfect age to take part in the military response to the Japanese attack on Pearl Harbor. Twenty years old and ready to go. The Marine recruiter gave me the choice of immediately being a "grunt" or finishing another year of college and going for flight school. Flight school it would be.

Chapter 1
Preflight School, St. Mary's College, California

After having survived the rigorous physical exams required to be considered a Naval Air Cadet, and having completed the required two years of college, the first stop was a pre-flight school in St. Mary's College in California. Physical conditioning took up about 60% of our time, and Naval History plus Elementary Navigation filled out the day.

Additionally a few of us who had played football were called upon to provide scrimmage fodder for the best football team in the country, the St. Mary's Pre-Flight varsity. The varsity was comprised of those professionals and All-Americans who had been drafted for instructor purposes in physical conditioning classes and/or playing football. As a sop for these monsters, they were granted immediate commissions in the Navy.

For some reason they had only a couple of centers, so though a volunteer for the service, I could not avoid the draft for football. In those days a center on offense always was a linebacker on defense. It was a terrible physical mismatch, and nightly horror dreams would recall seeing 260 pound Bugdanovicz pull out of his guard position looking for the 152 pound tiger of a linebacker. One time trying to take him on was enough. From that point on, finesse was the key to survival.

Some names come to mind. Frankie Albert *(the father of the T Formation)* was at quarterback, then there was a Bobby Grayson, and a Vic Bottari also in the backfield. Both were All-Americans from somewhere. Occasionally it was the assignment of Ed Manske *(all-pro Chicago Bears end)* to seek out that vicious linebacker. To avoid that collision required very deft footwork. Nightly I'd ask Tex Oliver after scrimmage if they hadn't had any centers check in that day, and remind him that there was a terrible mismatch here. His response, "You're doing fine, Andy, and we've got to have a center."

The happiest day of pre-flight school was when a big raw-boned lad from Texas checked in. He had played center at the university there. Whether he ever lived to graduate from St. Mary's is unknown to me, but for his arrival I was forever grateful.

We were told that two out of three would never make it through to graduation, and even in pre-flight school the weaning process had begun. There were those who were afraid to swing on a rope over deep pools, some wouldn't jump from a ten meter tower into the pool *(I didn't really blame them)*, and some even got tired of being tortured by gorilla professional wrestlers, who presumably were demonstrating the art of self defense. The next phase, whatever that may be, had to be better.

Chapter 2
Basic Flight Training, Livermore, California

Basic flight training at Livermore, CA, was truly a delight. First off, one had to be introduced to the Stearman N2S, a two cockpit, 235 H.P. round engine, fabric covered, yellow biplane which was to be the training room for the next few months.

Ground school now consisted of basic principles of flight, more Naval History, and some serious navigation. And, oh yes, Nomenclature. That was really fun. The object was to learn to identify, quickly, any ship at sea or any plane in the air. It started slowly, studying the characteristics and performance data on each object. Then, in a darkened room, the instructor would say, "Ready! Now!" and then flash on the screen a picture of anything, and we would record what we saw. In the beginning the flash would be about one second in length. As the class progressed, the time of exposure would gradually be reduced to 1/75th of a second. Generally the object was a plane or a ship but occasionally they'd throw in a stack of barrels, or a flock of birds, anything in odd numbers. The viewer would not only be called upon to identify the objects, but also give a count. Fun class, held every day.

Flight School was the primary reason for being here, and the skills were labeled as A,B,C,D. Each division had specific, measurable maneuvers to perform, and each was closed by a check ride with an unknown instructor. It was at this point that the weaning process began in earnest. One could move through the different stages at different speeds, so the semblance of a "class" deteriorated rapidly. Whether it took two or three "Down" checks to be sent home I do not know, but I think that further practice was allowed at least one time in each of the stages before a second check ride was given to allow passing through to the next stage.

The performance of the various maneuvers was great fun, and the performance vehicle could not have been better designed. The N2S could, and did, absorb unbelievable punishment. The airport had no runways, just a huge rectangular pad of asphalt. Planes would be taking off and/or landing to the right and left of one's own quivering platform. Sometimes a landing was attempted on top of another plane either landing or taking off. One can't see directly below. Yes, we lost some that way.

Stages A, B and C adequately prepared one for most right-side-up situations. Graceful, yet precise maneuvers such as the Chandelles and wing-overs, side-slips to a small circle, emergency landings, cross-country flights, and even night landings without lights. Simulated carrier landings at night between smudge pots claimed the careers of a few more would-be fly birds.

Stage D, the last barrier to advanced flight training using military type aircraft, proved to be the most fun of all. Right-side-up gave way to inverted flight. One was given to understand that, not only was it a thrill to level the wings with the horizon at the top of a loop while hanging from a seatbelt, it was a requirement. Occasionally a student would forget to fasten the seatbelt and fall out of the plane at the top of a loop or perhaps an Immelmann. If the parachute worked, that was a sure way of getting to see the old girl friend.

The acrobatics continued to be more demanding and exhilarating; the split-S, the slow roll, the violent snap roll. Very few planes are designed to withstand the forces of a snap roll, but the N2S could take it if the pilot could. Perhaps the most fun and most demanding of all was an instrument test in which the student was under a hood, while the instructor was

Stearman N2S Ground School Trainer
"unbelievably rugged workhorse"

uncovered in his cockpit. To consider the vast array of instruments in the Stearman is almost a joke. Spread across the instrument panel was an air speed indicator, a needle-ball, and mounted above the panel was a compass. All other instruments were engine related. The object of the lesson then, was to see if the student could right the plane, using only needle-ball and airspeed, after the instructor had gone through a series of violent maneuvers and suddenly called, "You've got it." He may have left the plane in a steep dive, perhaps heading straight up, maybe stalled out and upside down, or any other attitude which his imagination might concoct. The secret to solving the riddle was, in this sequence, center the needle, center the ball, and control the airspeed. One's brain, one's sense of balance and direction scream out that those three instruments are wrong, and it takes severe discipline and determination to fight those instincts and follow the direction of those instruments.

I was fortunate in stage D to have, as a daily instructor, the most feared check ride instructor on the base. In his Arkansas drawl he had said, "I'll have to give you a down check" more often than any instructor on the base. He was the best pilot I've ever known, and could do things with an airplane that others would not even attempt. On an otherwise uneventful day he mused, "Andy, how would you like to try an inverted falling leaf?" Inverted? I'd never seen one done properly right-side-up. Talk about a violent maneuver, this has to be the ultimate. And to Blackie *(his name was Blackshire)* this was just another way of having fun in an airplane that, thankfully, was designed to satisfy his whims of the moment.

Perhaps a year later, unbeknownst to me at the time, he saved my life. Having graduated, and having served a stint at Midway I ran into him at Eva, the Marine air base on Oahu. We were on our way to the Gilberts, and he had left the instructor ranks to join an F4U fighter squadron heading for the South Pacific. As always, his mind was on flying, and over a couple of drinks that night he posed the question:

"Andy, what's the most dangerous thing about dive bombing?"

The response of course, was "Finding yourself inverted in a high speed stall when pulling out of a dive." "That's right", he says, and what do you do about it?"

There really wasn't much to respond, because to my knowledge no one had ever survived such a thing, so my feeble response was, "Just be careful and try to avoid it."

"Nah," he drawled, "you have to anticipate the worst and plan exactly what to do in such an event, so that when the time comes you've already practiced your actions. There isn't time to figure out an escape when the unexpected occurs."

He went on to explain that he had given it a great deal of thought, and was pretty sure that his plan would work, but that surely no one would volunteer to give it a try. He was right. It did work, and to my knowledge I'm the only dive bomber pilot who has ever recovered from a high speed stall at pull-out. There are only two natural responses to finding yourself upside down at about 500 feet, with dive flaps open and no flying speed. First, one may try to roll right side up. That's not possible, there is not enough speed to turn over. Secondly, one might try to recover by pulling through as one would normally do in a split-S. That won't work either. Not enough altitude, nor enough speed with the flaps open. So, Blackie had theorized that if one could apply full throttle, push the stick all the way forward to try to keep the nose up while upside down, and immediately start to close the flaps in small increments as quickly as air speed would allow, all the time heading for the water, but using that five hundred feet to gain as much speed as possible, it was just barely possible that, just before entering the water, one might have gained enough speed to push the nose up a little farther, and slowly do a half roll. Crazy thought? Maybe. However, a lot of mental practice before it finally did occur saved the necessary milli-seconds to allow it to work. He was later shot down and killed by ground fire. His adversaries don't know how lucky they were. In air combat they wouldn't have had a chance. God rest his soul.

Chapter 3
Advanced Flight Training, Corpus Christi, Texas

Next stop was Corpus Christi, the last leg. Survival here meant a commission in either the Navy or the Marine Corps. The training was identical. Two qualifications to be commissioned as a Marine were:
      a. Be in the top ten percent of the graduating class
      b. Volunteer
These then were my two goals.

The first introduction to a military type, metal, low wing, round engine plane was to the SNV, the Vultee vibrator. It was a terrible airplane, yet I still recall the exhilaration I felt on the first solo flight in this rattle trap. It was fixed gear and couldn't really do anything but fly straight and in circles. In it, however, I experienced my first instructor who would like to have bounced me out of the program. By that time, though, the Navy had a great deal of money invested in each cadet, and hopefully, the weaning process would be slowed considerably.

1941 Vultee SNV-1 (BT13-A) Vibrator
"the worst of all trainers"

It was the first flight, and I met the instructor at the plane with a "Good morning, sir."

His response was simply, "Get in." Then, over the headset, "Do you think you can start this thing?"

"Yes sir."

After a brief warm-up *(I had spent an hour the evening before just sitting in the cockpit familiarizing myself with the controls and instruments)*, with no further word from the guy in the other seat, I signaled the crew chief to pull the wheel chocks and started to taxi out to the end of the runway. Just think, here we had runways instead of that huge rectangle. First class, I'm thinking, to be able to taxi to the end of a runway, to actually have a two-way radio with which one could request clearance from the tower, and take-off in some kind of order.

These thoughts were rudely interrupted by someone screaming in the headset, "Turn this Goddamn thing around and park. I'll tell you when it's time to go, and until then you sit there and listen for the instructions."

After parking in the same spot I let it run until he screamed, "Don't you even know how to shut the damned thing off?"

"Yes sir."

After I crawled out of the cockpit and got down on the ground where he could address me eye to eye, he continued to berate not only me, but all of the stupid cadets who were sent to him, and it was no wonder we were losing the war and God help all of those who may have to deal with me in the future. This tirade had to take no less than five minutes before he finally let me go with "I hope to hell I never have to see you again." He didn't. Apparently, he requested that stupid S.O.B. be assigned to someone else, and his superior gratefully *(for my sake)* complied.
Next day with a different instructor, we flew around a bit, had a nice familiarization tour of the different fields, some instructions on traffic patterns, etc., and I was okayed for solo in this bucket of bolts.

Thankfully, after just a few days in the SNV, I was transferred to one of the outlying fields, I think it was Cabaniss, for dive-bombing training. This time we got to fly a real airplane, the North American SNJ. This was a low wing, round engine, 450 HP dandy with retractable gear. There are still many of them flying today, used in air shows, races, and movies about WWII. They're dolled up to represent our side as well as the Japanese. A truly class airplane.

North American AT-6 / SNJ Texan, advanced trainer, Army Air Corps and U.S. Navy: The Pilot Maker.
"a beautiful, powerful, trainer to equip one for any warplane"

All of the flying here was solo. Much time was spent on formation flying, always in sections of three and divisions of six. In the Navy or Marine world, formation flying means putting your wing tip inside of the wing tip of the leading plane, close enough to read the lips of the neighboring pilot. One learns to stay there through some rather stressful maneuvers; tight turns, even gentle roll-overs. Confidence in the lead plane is essential, and for that pilot, smooth flying is a prime requisite. Fortunately, most of my time was spent as a lead plane of a section, which then could mean leader of a division, or lead plane of a squadron. All orders were given by either head or hand signals, just a nod signaling to add or ease up on the throttle, to turn, or to climb. For more extended communication, sometimes the Morse code was employed by tapping one's head with either a fist or extended fingers, the fist meaning "dit", and extended fingers a "dah".

Each of the SNJs was equipped with one 30 caliber machine gun, and much of our time was spent on gunnery. There is a great deal of difference in technique between Army training and Navy training in gunnery. Essentially an Army pilot seeks to get on the tail of his target and gun him down. The Navy or Marine pilots specialize in deflection shooting, coming in at a sharp angle to the moving target regardless of the direction of approach. So, Kentucky windage is applied from whatever angle. The preferred approach would be from overhead, making a dive which almost is a collision approach, but passing just behind the tail of the target after delivering a short burst of bullets from overhead giving plenty of lead. Just like shooting ducks. In fact, one of the things we did quite a lot of on the ground was to practice skeet shooting. Great training for deflection shooting.

Our target was a white fabric sock, probably a couple feet in diameter towed by a rope from another plane. Each of us in the training section *(usually six at a time)* had bullets whose tips had been dipped in different colors of paint. At the end of the flight we could count bullet holes in the sock and know how many hits each of us had. Twice I severed the rope just ahead of the sock. Both times the tow pilot was able to gently pick the falling sock out of the sky on his wing tip and bring it safely back to earth.

Various approaches were used in this exercise. Overhead, from either side, or from directly below. In each case one started parallel to the target, but well ahead in order to allow a 180 degree turn to face the target from various altitude differences. In direct collision approach, one lowered the nose to get below the target, and then nose up in time to give a lead, but still avoid collision. Rather precise timing judgment was required.

The latter collision approach brings to mind the experience of Jack Congor, a Marine fighter pilot who had run out of ammunition in his aerial combat with Japanese Zeroes. He maneuvered his F4U into a direct frontal approach, ducked under the nose of his adversary, pulled up and cut off the tail of the Zero with his propeller. Unbelievable timing, considering the closing speed of the two planes had to be in excess of 600 mph. Both pilots parachuted into the ocean where Jack was picked up by a friendly dingy launched by a larger boat. He directed that they also pick up the other pilot. As Jack held out his hand to help him into the boat, the Jap suddenly stuck a pistol in Jack's face and pulled the trigger. Luckily it didn't fire. Jack fell back, grabbed a docking hook and split the head of his opponent. Sometimes justice is served.

One could not really practice dive-bombing in an SNJ as it had no diving flaps to slow the aircraft in a dive. Glide bombing was the best we could do. That was performed at about a 45 degree angle and with not too much altitude, to prevent exceeding the speed limits of the airframe. The practice bombs were small smoke bombs to allow us to see the point of impact. Targets ranged from circles painted on the ground to smoke bombs dropped in the water to small armor plated boats engaged in evasive tactics.

After a few months of intensive two-a-day flights, plus rigorous ground school in navigation and nomenclature it was time to graduate. The purchase of uniforms was required, so a day off to go to Corpus Christi and order a pair of greens and a pair of khakis was all that was required. At that time the traditional Marine bell-hop red, white, and blue uniform was not a requirement. It was just as well. There was little time for the greens or khakis, and all of the day to day uniforms were supplied free. Strange, after the graduation ceremony, to be wearing the bars of a second lieutenant, and have enlisted men salute as they approached. It seems we had been saluting first forever. Nice to have pockets too. They had been sewed up for months to help train us to keep our hands out of our pockets.

A proud Marine Second Lieutenant

Chapter 4
Post Graduate Training, Florida

The first assignment as a trained pilot was someplace in Florida, where we flew OS2U's. OS designated "Observation Scout," and the U stood for the manufacturer, Vaught Sikorsky. Vaught's claim to fame was the F4U fighter, the best in the business, but it surely wasn't the OS2U. The OS2U was designed as a Scout plane to be launched from Cruisers or Battleships, and then to land in the wake of the ship and be plucked back aboard with a little crane. For any other purpose it was a joke. Ours were, of course, on fixed wheels instead of floats, but otherwise the same.

An OS2U-1 at the Naval Aircraft Factory, 1941   "amazing to remain airborne at such slow speed"

The first shock came when starting the round engine for the first time. In the cockpit was an ingenious device which looked like a giant loading mechanism for a bolt action rifle. Into this receptacle one would insert a shell about three or four times the size of a 10 gauge shotgun shell. When the ground crew captain assured the propeller was clear, he shouted, "Clear" and the pilot pulled the trigger. The smoke in the cockpit after the explosion obscured all of the instruments, but if the engine had indeed started, the noise and vibration assured the pilot that the first step to flying was successful.

After graduation, we never again had dual instruction in an airplane. One would spend as much time as necessary in the cockpit for familiarization, and then fly the thing. All instruction given was by a seasoned pilot in another plane. Again we would practice formation, always formation when more than one plane was involved. I don't think the OS2U even had a gun, but it did have a scope through the windshield through which one would peer when trying to line up on a bombing run. It was in this relic that I first experienced engine failure. Just after take-off from a swamp surrounded runway, it fired its last piston. Why it didn't nose over as I put it down between tree stumps in the mud is somewhat of a mystery. The only logical reason is that it was so slow it didn't have the kinetic energy to do the trick.

Maybe a month later, a welcome move to some other field in Florida found me getting an introduction to yet another Vaught product, the SB2U. "SB" signifies a scout bomber, which also serves as a dive bomber. By now, the cockpit explosion required to start the engine was old hat, and this fabric fuselage, metal winged lady even had retractable gear. Now we're getting someplace. There was one thing, though. After take-off the wheels retracted straight back into the wheel wells in the wings. The wheel alignment, however, rotated ninety degrees during retraction to allow them to fit flat in the wings. Again the engineers at Vaught Sikorsky proved their ingenuity. Instead of providing diving flaps for the dive bomber to control the speed during a dive, it was decided to lower the wheels and simply not rotate them on the supporting gear. This would provide a flat-plate area which would serve as the diving brake. It did slow the dive somewhat, though the speed continued to build for the duration of the dive, and the controls became more and more immovable as the speed increased.

SB2Us were what we had when the war started, along with a few SBDs. The major problem with the landing gear arrangement occurred during landing rather than in a dive. Occasionally a pilot would lower the wheels to "dive' mode rather than "landing" mode. The resulting nose over was rather embarrassing, but those

SB2U Vindicator in flight over Hawaii, c. 1941. "great range if one could survive the smoke in the cockpit"

wheels just wouldn't roll very well when facing the wrong direction. The scope through the windshield proved to be a problem. One could easily become transfixed looking through the scope and lose track of altitude. The SB2U wouldn't pull out very quickly, so we lost some who waited a little too long to begin the pull-out.

We were again met with the SB2U challenge when we reported to Chicago to check out on carrier landings and take-offs. That was fun. One either liked and could easily time the starting approach, or hated it. Fortunately, for me, it was most enjoyable, and placing full confidence in the landing officer was not a problem, For some, it was a nightmare. We had one nose–over on the deck by a pilot who missed the landing cables, and there were those who were still there trying to get checked out when I left for San Diego.

Perhaps a few words should be said here about the "mood" of the country at that time. The "mood" was certainly one of unity, beyond what we have ever experienced since. That "mood" included a most charitable feeling for service men of all types, and, it seemed to me, especially for Marine pilots. While in Chicago checking out on carriers, we did a tour of State Street one night, and it was impossible to buy a drink. When entering a bar the cries came out, "Hey Marine! Over here!" We were flooded with offers of drinks. Not only drinks but women. Most of the men were in the service, so not only were men rare, but Marine pilots, I guess, were considered a rare find.

My upbringing did not include violating women. Dad had always told me that, "A man is like a piece of old pottery. You can break it many times, glue it together, and not much damage is done. A woman, however, is different. She's like a piece of fine China. Once it's broken, the cracks will always be visible." So, though completely out of character, my stock in trade response came to be, "Get away from me woman. Liquor's my weakness."

I don't think that at that time there were any of us who thought we would return to the states alive, once we left for the Pacific. Each of us was "living it up for today" in his own way. Though each of us had his own faults, lack of patriotism was not one of them. There were no draftees in Marine Air. I was roundly ridiculed and teased about my letting all of those women go, but honestly, they held little appeal. McSpad (*so named because his dad flew Spads in WWI*) used to say, "Andy, this is like going through a candy factory. Take your pick." But then, I had never had anything to drink through two years of college either, so I was enjoying that instead.

Finally we were rewarded with SBDs, the best operational dive bomber of WWII. This all metal doll had dive flaps which would maintain a speed not to exceed 220 mph regardless of the duration of the dive. And, throughout the dive the controls remained free and easy so one could rotate as required all during the dive. The scope through windshield had been replaced by a prism sight which projected a circle and a dot somewhere out front. The wheels were mounted far enough outboard on the wings to allow retraction inboard without rotation. Mounted in the cockpit, just above the instrument panel, were two 50 caliber machine guns, synchronized to fire between the prop blades of the three bladed propeller. Like most mechanical things, the timing at times failed, and holes would be blasted through the propeller. The resulting vibration was severe if the number of holes in the blades was not equal, but to my knowledge it never brought a plane down.

From the SBD-1 to the SBD-6, Simply the Best!

One would think that with 1350 horsepower this thing might get up and go, but no way. Slow was the name of the game. The acronym SBD no longer referred to "Scout Bomber Douglas", but was replaced by "Slow But Deadly". That said, you would not find a more dependable plane. One SBD that I know of survived after 225 bullet holes. The SBD was to be the plane for all of my service overseas, and one couldn't have had a sturdier, more dependable partner.

Chapter 5
El Toro, California

The collection of pilots assembled at El Toro, the Marine air base close to Los Angeles, included very few that were known to me. Some 45 of us were assigned to become a new dive-bomber squadron. The skipper was a major who had been overseas, but had never seen any combat. There was one captain, the executive officer, who had never left the states, two or three first lieutenants who had been instructors, and the rest of us were second Louies just a couple of months out of flight school. Not one hour of combat experience in the group. Yet, when this crew was assembled, we were considered to be the squadron with the most hours of flight time that had ever been put together.

Most of us, the Second Lieutenants that is, had about five hundred hours flight time. The skipper had carefully hand-picked his non-commissioned group of sergeants to run this squadron, so there was a lot of experience there. None were pilots, but they were in charge of maintenance, ordinance, supplies, commissary, etc. Fortunately for us these non-coms were really qualified, because the skipper was an alcoholic whose judgment in all areas became worse as the day progressed.

At the time we left the states, the attrition rate of Marine dive-bomber pilots was so high that we were told to take the following collar bars with us from the states: First Lieutenant, Captain, Major, and Light Colonel. "Field" promotions were given on the spot to fill vacancies as they occurred. Some First Lieutenants were serving as squadron commanders. That seemed to be a terrible waste of money to a few of us. Obviously we wouldn't all need those bars, so we went together, purchased a bunch of bars, and one of the guys kept them in a place where we all had access to them. Come to think of it, I never asked where they were kept.

Eva was the re-grouping place for all Marine squadrons and pilots. We were not there long, but long enough to get to see some of the returnees from such battles as Guadalcanal and Midway. These were honest-to-God heroes who had shot down Zeroes, had sunk ships of the Jap fleet, and were here at the bar with the rest of us who were wondering what our reaction would be when first faced with those shots fired in anger.

Our first flight here in our new airplanes took us over Pearl Harbor, where numerous ships still lay on their sides, making sea lanes treacherous until they could be removed. Now, more than a year after the sneak attack, the evidence of the devastation was still everywhere to be seen. Thousands of our guys were still entombed in those ships. What had only been seen in newspapers and Movietone News had now become very real. This was a war, and we would soon become a part of it.

Heading for Oahu on the USS Coral Sea October, 1943

Chapter 6
Midway Island

Our first stop was to be the island of Midway, where the turning point battle of the war had been waged a few months before. We were to be transported by air with personal gear, and squadron gear would arrive by ship. Unfortunately, some of us made the trip in a C-46, a giant two engine transport built by Curtis. We were obviously overloaded. We sat on benches, with our backs to the outside of the fuselage. The center of the cabin was stacked with our gear. Each man had a foot locker, and these were randomly stacked between the two rows of pilots, along with our most precious possession, booze. Each of us had been allotted three cases of Seagrams VO for which we paid $50. These had been more carefully stacked.

One engine popped a couple of times as this monster labored to get off of the ground, but eventually we cleared the end of the runway at Eva and the pilot pointed the nose, hopefully, toward Midway. Whoa, it's a big ocean out there. A couple hours later it became a damned sight bigger when that one engine failed. This thing had all it could do to stay aloft with both engines, let alone one. The cargo door open, we unloaded the foot lockers one at a time. That helped, the angle of descent gradually lessened, but still we were losing altitude. Until now, it had simply been a matter of survival. Now, however, we were considering earthly pleasures, and tears became numerous as, one by one, the cases of VO were gently tossed through the cargo door.

I had perused a map before this trip, and saw nothing but water between the Hawaiian Islands and Midway, but suddenly the guy in the co-pilot seat was talking about French Frigate Shoal. Hopefully, he knew what he was talking about, because there was nothing left to throw overboard, and we were still losing altitude at a modest rate. Have you ever seen a man earnestly kissing a strip of coral sand? More than one of these fearless fly-boys knelt gently down on the landing strip at French Frigate

Shoals and gratefully tasted the coral.

What was a mechanic doing out there? Maybe the Pentagon had properly anticipated such an event, cause there he was. Some hours and tinkering later, we again lifted off, much lighter this time, and headed out in search of Midway. Again the kissing routine at the air strip on Eastern Island, Midway. This time, however, kissing space had to be purchased at the expense of some Gooney bird. There were thousands of them, in all directions; these Laysan Albatross claimed Midway as their part time home, and we were very unwelcome intruders.

There are two islands at Midway, Sand Island, the larger of the two, and Eastern Island, large enough for three runways. Each of the runways stretched from water to water, and all buildings *(Quonset Huts)* were carefully positioned between runways. The highest spots on the island were the tops of the piles of coral sand placed in a "U" formation around each plane for protection. These protective pilings were called "Revetments" and were to become our protective hangars from then on. Never again would planes be lined up on the parking aprons, or huddled together in hangars as was the case at Pearl Harbor. Between the two islands was a deep channel, protected by a net which prevented ships or subs from entering the protected waters of the atoll.

The coral atoll was probably ten miles in diameter, and the protected waters served as the major Pacific base for our submarine fleet. It was here that they came for re-fueling, food and supplies, more torpedoes, and some needed fresh air for the crew. All of this was performed at Sand Island, and we, on Eastern island provided their protection.

Each morning, before daylight, we found on the blackboard in the pilots' ready-room the name of the incoming subs, the latitude and longitude of emerging, and the time of surfacing. After volunteering to meet the sub, take-off was timed to allow the flight to arrive at the rendezvous point at the pre-arranged time.

Surfacing was always about thirty nautical miles from the island in any direction, and it was always a great thrill to see these leviathans nosing up out of the deep. About one complete circle overhead would allow enough time for a figure to emerge from the conning tower, and then flashing lights in Morse Code would establish identity of the sub. The gunner, seated behind the armor plate separating pilot and gunner, would by blinker lights establish our identity, and the trip on the surface to Midway was under way. Our job was to circle the sub at all times until safely in the harbor, watching for subs or torpedoes during the trip. Upon entrance between the islands as the net was displaced, it was very important to see that a trailing sub did not enter the protected waters. One of the great thrills in observing the activities at the conning tower, was to see the ritual of tying a sweep broom to the periscope. This didn't always happen, but when it did, it signaled the success of the crew in sinking a ship with each of the torpedoes fired.

It was a great place to practice navigation. The instruments involved were the compass, the airspeed indicator, and a plotting board residing under the instrument panel on a drawer slide. The key to success was the ability to judge not only the direction, but the velocity of the wind by looking at the water below. In the classroom, wind velocity and speed were always a given part of the problem. Seldom, in the classroom, did the wind change from time to time. Because of the vital importance of judgment of wind, one would never fly over 100 feet above the water. On a regular basis, we would be asked to provide cover for a small convoy going past. A single plane would leave Midway, rendezvous with the convoy, then circle the ships watching for subs. After a few hours, when low on fuel, the plane would head for home.

Tricky! Upon joining up with the convoy, one no longer navigated the position of the plane, but began tracking the convoy position. Now, one must judge the speed of the ships by the wake, and track their direction without regard for the wind. This, while the ships changed heading regularly to avoid being tracked by subs. We couldn't very well ask for help from the tower in Midway without disclosing the position of the convoy. The Japs certainly knew where Midway was but hopefully, not the position of the convoy. So, not all planes found their way home.

Each morning found us up having breakfast long before dawn. As an aside, because of this being a major Naval base, the food was very good, and I guess in retrospect, we just assumed we'd always be well fed. We'd see. The reason for the early get-up time was to get to the planes, each protected in its own revetment of coral, fire up the engines to be warmed up and ready to go by dawn.

Wake Island, far to the west, had already fallen to the Japanese, and Tokyo Rose reminded us regularly that we were to be next. Each day, including Sunday, after what happened at Pearl Harbor, every plane was ready, with a pilot in the cockpit, until about an hour after sunrise. No night flights were attempted there. The meteorologists had told us that, for some reason, this was the darkest spot on the earth. It seemed to be true. At night, if there was no moon, one had to use a flashlight to find his Quonset hut. There was no horizon visible, and as a consequence, pilots had simply rolled over and augured into the ocean after take-off in night attempts.

The Gooney birds provided the only entertainment during the stay there, and they were a riot. We did have to set 500 feet as Gooney Bird altitude, and never retract the landing gear until above that. They were so big that if jammed into the wheel well upon retraction, the hydraulics were not powerful enough to lower the gear. A direct hit during flight resulted in severe damage to the leading edge of the wing, or in a few cases, even smashed the windshield of the cockpit. Their antics in the air and on the ground have supplied the subject matter for complete

Baby Gooney watching

Gooney wingspan　　　　　　　　*All dark Gooney babies*

books, so no attempt will be made to duplicate that here. Suffice it to say we were fortunate to be there during mating season and the hatch of the little Goonies.

Not only was the island known for the Gooney birds, but it was a bird sanctuary for everything from the tiny Kiwi bird *(who couldn't fly)* to the giant Frigate bird, sporting a wingspan of ten feet. There was a red, white, and blue curiosity that would fly backward over the length of the island at about eight feet in altitude facing into the wind, and then proceed to walk back to the upwind shore to repeat the journey. Thankfully these feathered friends provided the necessary entertainment relief because no woman had ever been on the island, nor were they allowed. So, the only USO Show we ever saw there was Eddie Peabody with his banjo.

Darkness usually signaled the time to grab a flashlight and head for the Officers' Club. It, too, was a Quonset hut, furnished with a bar, a bartender, a few couches, tables, and two pool tables. The skipper would, by now, be totally snockered. Oftentimes he would be sitting in the couch facing the door awaiting my arrival. We had always had a pool table in the basement of our house for my dad and his cronies, so I was better than most at pool, though not really enamored of the game. Upon my arrival he would stagger to his feet and announce, "We'll challenge any two of you here!" Perhaps that was why I took to practicing throwing knives in the barracks Quonset hut at night instead of going to the club. Entertainment was hard to come by.

An early indication of the status of our skipper was a meeting he called one night for all pilots in the ready room. The only door was secured by two armed guards, spaced far enough from the entrance so they could not hear what went on inside. When all were seated, the Major softly announced, "Gentlemen, we're going to take Wake." That made sense. We would welcome the chance to be a part of liberating the Marines held in prisons there.

Then he proceeded to reveal the details of the plan. Our squadron was to be picked up by a carrier and transported to the island. Each of us was to carry a loaded carbine, plus the pistol on our belts, in the cockpit of the aircraft when we launched. We were to land on Wake, taxi rapidly to the end of the runway and with the help of our rear seat gunner with his twin 30 calibers, establish a beachhead at the end of the runway. The ground Marines would then land and back us up.

We were not to tell anyone of the plan, nor even to discuss it with one another, as it was feared that the enlisted men would mutiny if they got any word of the plan. Crazy? Of course! Would the Navy really do this? What the hell did we know about establishing a beachhead? Yet something about the secrecy with which the plan was revealed seemed to lend some measure of credibility to this wild scheme. For days we looked at each other sideways, wondering if suddenly here would be an order to take off and land aboard some carrier. Obviously he was cracking up, but we weren't that sure until later.

Chapter 7
Makin Island

After about three months of Midway we were replaced by another squadron. So, back to Eva *(this time uneventfully)* for regrouping. We loaded up on another Jeep carrier with a deck load of brand new SBDs and headed for somewhere. Majuro was the next stop. Here in the Gilberts we found ourselves within striking distance of four Japanese held islands. Striking distance for an SBD wasn't very far away.

First thing, we had to get these spotless SBDs off of this little carrier. So, while anchored in the harbor in Majuro a Navy pilot came aboard and gave us instructions for taking off with a catapult. "Hold your head hard back against the head-rest so your head doesn't snap off," he says, "and lock your elbow against a solid rib in the cockpit once you get full throttle. Otherwise, you'll chop the throttle when they fire the catapult."

So, after that indoctrination, we climbed aboard and taxied, one by one, to our place over the catapult hook on the deck. Normally, the carrier would be under way heading into the wind for this procedure thus adding about 30 knots or more to the airspeed for take-off. Here, we were anchored in the lagoon, so upon firing, the plane would dip almost into the water before having enough speed to fly. All made it safely, however, so where to now? Obviously we couldn't remain here, the accommodations were much too good... Quonset huts for every twenty of us.

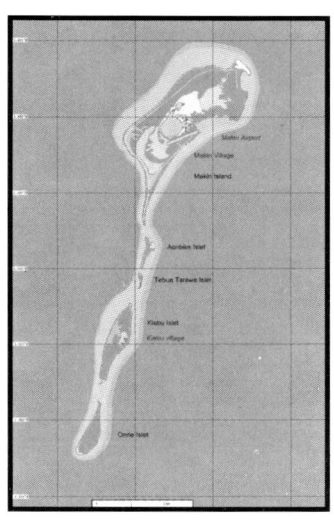

A small dot in the Pacific (for larger version refer to page 78)

So, now that Carlson's Raiders had neutralized Makin, it looked like the perfect spot to train us in more Spartan surroundings. For this trip to Makin, I was assigned to handle the enlisted men, and we were to be transported by destroyer. There's not enough room on a destroyer for the crew, let alone 150 enlisted men. Thankfully, most of them were sick for the short trip, so discipline was not to be a problem. The executive officer on board was one of the most slender men I've ever met. He confided to me that he'd been sick every day of his tour on this can, but the Navy would not listen to any requests for transfer.

A destroyer is so named because of its mission. It is built as a sub-chaser. It is small, as Navy ships go, very maneuverable and very fast. When, during the trip, a sub alert sounded, this thing, with 150 sick Marines aboard, took off like a speed boat. Immediately all gun positions were manned, men were at the ready at the depth-charge stations, and all below deck operations were manned and ready. It was hoped this would not be a false alarm, as it would have been fun to see the firing of the depth charges and the actions of the crew. It was not to be. The "All Clear" sounded, and our men were again afforded their places at the rail as we continued the trip to Makin.

The Locals

The only people left on Makin were the natives, and they were missing most all of the young girls. The Japs had taken them with them as they fled. The Seabees were there, firming up the airstrip with those perforated, interlocking metal strips that reminded one of erector set components. They did make for a fast, but rough, usable runway. The coral strip was wide enough for a single runway and farther down widened out enough to allow us to set up a tent city for housing.

Makin - home for 10 months

We set up our own tents, using those same erector set strips for flooring. The tents were large enough for four bunks, but normally we had only three per tent and used the fourth corner for personal gear and booze. When each cot had been fitted with a mosquito net and a large tent had been erected to serve as a mess tent, we were declared operational.

The mess tent sort of divided the camp between enlisted quarters and officers' quarters. Their tents were the same as ours. There was one large latrine for officers which accommodated many at a time, where we would have time to discuss world problems and the agenda of the day. Additionally, in that this was before gender integration, there were many "Pee Tubes" randomly located along pathways where one could at any time find relief. These were simply funnels placed on top of a pipe sunk in the coral ground. That must have been deemed more sanitary than simply relieving oneself between the trees.

Makin was uniquely positioned in the middle of four Japanese-held islands, each of which boasted an airfield. The Naval strategy, though never explained to us, was to bypass many of these Jap-held islands rather than to pay the enormous price of invasion of each. Tarawa, Iwo Jima, Saipan, etc. had exacted a toll of thousands of Marines. Some of these islands were critical steps on the route to Japan, but many others could be neutralized and then bypassed. Such was the case for our four neighbors: Mille, Wotje, Maloelap and Jaluit. Our assignment, then, was to destroy, in sequence, the airfield, gun emplacements, control centers and ammunition dumps. Perhaps we deviated from that priority list at times, but, though unexplained, it seemed to be the normal order. In addition, we were to see to it that no supply ships, surface or subs, were able to reach any of the four.

To best satisfy this assignment, our squadron of 45 pilots was divided into two groups, and each group would fly every other day. We actually flew more often than that, because in addition to the scheduled bombing strikes of the day, four planes were required for search of the neighboring islands both morning and night. However, we still managed quite a few days off. A full complement for a strike would be 24 planes or three divisions. Seldom did we have that many planes flying, but we stayed above 18 most of the time.

It was about this time that the skipper called all of the pilots together to give us hell because not one of us had performed his assigned duties. Truth is, none of us knew what he was talking about. We were fly-boys, and had been flying almost every day, so what was his problem?

He asserted that he had posted a list of duties for each officer, and sure enough there was a list up there at this time. Each of us had duties such as: "Personnel Officer", "Commissary Officer", "Flight Officer", "Ordinance Officer", etc. Fortunately, my duty was "Engineering Officer". A visit with Van Boskirk (*funny how some names come back*), a master sergeant who knew everything there was to know about an SBD, who had built up a massive inventory of parts and who was so mean he had frightened a great deal of competency into his collection of line mechanics, left me feeling totally inadequate. He informed me that the only thing he couldn't do was fly the damned things. He could, of course, if he wanted to, but he wasn't that damned stupid. So, I became the test pilot for any airframe that had been particularly damaged or for any engine after severe damage or overhaul. A great job! It was also a job the skipper wanted no part of.

Chapter 8
Shots Fired!

We're about to find out how we'll respond when we see those first bursts of flak around us. How will it be in a dive with tracers going by? Is it true that you never see the one that hits you? How will one's wingmen respond, or one's gunner? And lastly, after all of this training, will you hit the target or will you dump it in the ocean? These and many other questions interrupted one's sleep, along with the steady drone of mosquitoes. Then there were the giant sand crabs, huge things that ran sideways through the tent at night, sounding like a tractor running over all that metal. Still, come morning, the sound of that engine was a great wake-up call, and one couldn't help but be excited and eager to go.

A couple of hours later, after continued laboring for altitude, the target, Mille, was in sight, and we had about 12,000 feet to squander to get to the target for the day. The target was a piece of cake, just dismantle the runways. Funny, the sky now had a bunch of small black clouds at about our altitude which hadn't been there before. We nosed over a little to pick up some speed between here and where we'd roll over into a dive. Also, we did engage in some evasive tactics, still being careful to be very smooth in deference to those wingmen. Arm the bombs, roll over into a dive, and now one could see where those black clouds were coming from. Bright flashes from gun emplacements all over the island gave away the positions of their big guns, then as one got lower, the different staccato flashes of 40 millimeter and 20 mm rapid fire machine guns replaced the large flashes of the 90 millimeter guns which had greeted our arrival. These smaller weapons, though also with explosive heads, left some streams of tracers. Rather pretty. Fourth of July kind of thing!

Then, keep one eye on the altimeter, the large hand rapidly unwinding, and as it passes 1000 feet pull the release, get out of the dive, head for the water, cross controls, and skid from one side to the other, hoping the gunners on the ground will take the bait and lead you in the direction the plane appears to be traveling. Hopefully, by the time he gets it figured out you'll be out of range. Careful, also, not to get too close to the water; some of the larger shells put up quite a water wall which one wouldn't want to fly through. Now, then, where's the skipper? We have to join up and head for home. How in the hell did he get up to 6000 feet already? Obviously, he unloaded from up there. We even made up a song about him:

"I'm a pilot true from old Snafu and I haven't any sense,
I climb into my SBD and then I do commence.
I drop my bombs on Mille, from clouds up in the sky,
And I pull out at 6000 feet cause the ack ack is so high."

By now it was clear to all that he had cracked up. His replacement was a former heavyweight professional fighter. Rumor had it that he had been sent overseas to prevent him from having to stand court martial for throwing another officer down the stairs of an officers' club, and then throwing a slot machine down on top of him. Whether or not that was true I don't know, but his mean streak would surely have allowed it to happen. His leadership technique was most unique. If any man, officer or enlisted, gave any trouble, he was invited out into the woods to see who would emerge as the leader. By the time I returned to the states, over a year later, his leadership had never been challenged to my knowledge.

For his first few flights, he never led the squadron. He flew in the last section, turned the lead over to one of the section leaders, and observed the actions of all of the pilots. One of his most interesting philosophies surfaced at an early meeting.

" I don't want any of you guys becoming buddies," he snarled. "First thing you know, you'll be moping around here 'cause your buddy is gone. Goddamn it, that's what you're here for."

For the most part I could follow that advice. Truth is, it was very good advice, although it seemed rather cruel at the time. We were not at all close-knit unless flying. There were quite a few that I plain disliked, a few that I warmed to, but most were just names, most of which escape me by now. One of the good guys later turned out to be a brother-in-law. And, fortunately for me, a tent-mate, Sam, did turn out to be a good friend. Fortunately, we never had to go around mourning the loss of either.

Every squadron had one officer trained in the infantry as a ground officer. Our first one was a kook. During the day, he always wore shorts, short sleeved shirts, and clodhopper high shoes. His uniform of the day was a pith helmet, no shirt, shorts, belt with loaded '45 pistol, and his clodhopper high shoes. In this uniform he could normally be found jumping rope, punching a bag, or jogging, sweating profusely all the time. I always thought he would challenge the skipper, but he never did. What he did do on some of these jogs was to find, capture, and incarcerate one or two Japanese who had, for one reason or another, failed to leave the island. These few shed their uniforms, threw on a grass skirt, moved in with the natives, and defied us to find them. Old what's his name would spot them by observing their footprints in the sand. The Japs had a wide space between the big toe and the next one because of the sandals they had worn. The natives print looked like a bear paw. So, we had a little jail. The Japs would scowl as we walked by, but they were better fed than they had ever been.

Now all of us would like to have had the opportunity to go back home to visit the family, wives, girl friends, or whomever we left behind. What's his name, however, had a greater urge than most, and sought to satisfy that urge by commandeering a landing barge one night, loading it up with survival gear, and heading off for the states. He figured he had served enough time here, and was damned if he was going to await his replacement. Some Navy ship picked him up, brought him back, and satisfied his urge to be sent back to the states. His replacement was considerably more rational, but those ground officers were trained to be killers, and were somewhat different.

Chapter 9
Guard Duty

On the island, by now, was a battalion of blacks. *(There was no integration at that time)*. I don't really know what they did, but I think they were some kind of maintenance group. At any rate, some of their group was always employed to unload ships as they came in. If the cargo was destined for our squadron, a couple of us would be called upon to supervise the unloading. Keep in mind here that we were trained to be fly-boys. One such day, I was assigned the afternoon shift to supervise the unloading of a hold full of beer. When I arrived, some of the unloading crew appeared about half snockered. There was nothing very sophisticated about the unloading. They simply formed a line, and each would pick up a case of beer as they descended into the hold, carry it up and out another passageway and deposit the case on a truck. Down below, however, they had broken open cases as desired, and would help themselves to a beer now and then. When finished, back into the trudge line.

My predecessor had apparently never been below, or if so, wanted to be a good guy and forget it. For whatever reasons, military discipline demanded more than that of me, so I headed below to observe the proceedings. As my eyes became accustomed to the semi-darkness, a huge, shirtless, sweating black man stood up behind a stack of beer cases. An NFL scout would have drooled at the sight of this fellow. There was no fat, just a great specimen of a man, with arms and torso of steel, and in one hand a bottle of beer being raised to his lips. I drew my '38 revolver, pointed it at him, and then heard myself say, "If you take a swig of that beer I'll kill you." Did that come out of me? Then the stare down. I'm sure he was thinking, "There's no way this kid is going to shoot me for taking a swig of beer... or will he?" Frankly, I didn't know either, but I think I would have. Thank God I never had to find out.

Some moments later, still staring at me, he slowly placed the bottle on a case, threw another case on his shoulder and headed out. Never, for the rest of the afternoon, did I quit climbing up and down that ladder, watching every man and every case from hold to truck. Jobs like this should be for those infantry guys.

Chapter 10
War Games

The mindset of our adversary was certainly no surprise to us, but it was strikingly reinforced on a day after we had again bombed Mille. Unfortunately, the day before, we had lost one who had parachuted into the water, but very close to the shore. This day, for those whose bombing runs took them close to a runway intersection, the spectacle of our pilot staked out on the ground greeted them. He was placed right in the intersection of the runways. Another reason, perhaps, why it may take one more generation before all prejudice is erased.

Most of the intelligence officers I met were washed out cadets, and consequently, didn't like the pilots very much. Such was the case with "Sad Sack", our intelligence officer. I think he particularly disliked me, and if so, I returned the compliment. We would often have briefings, *(maybe always)* after a strike on some target, and each of us was asked where our bomb hit, etc. On this particular day, the weather was miserable, high winds, blowing in different directions on the way down, and the bombs were scattered in all directions. Nothing to be proud of. The target of the day was an ammunition bunker. After the strike, Sack started the questioning with the leader, and then went through each man in each section. I happened to be the leader of the third division, and in response to his query I said, "Yes, I hit it, but just on the one end."

"What makes you think so?"

"I always look back to see where I hit, and then confirm with my gunner."

He then proceeded to tell me that someone else must have hit it, but he didn't know who. The photos from the last plane confirmed what I had told him. But he hadn't yet found out whose bomb did the trick. My final shot was, "If you're going to figure it out anyway, why in the hell do you ask me?"

It's true that we had more booze than we should have, and that night it's true that I had more than I should have. After considerable thought on the subject, I went to Sack's tent and announced that I didn't like the way he ran the intelligence for this outfit, whereupon I picked up his cot and headed out for the ocean. He followed, pleading for me to bring his cot back, but I was headed for the reef. Finally, in water just deep enough to completely cover the cot, I gently placed it in the surf. Next morning someone came to our tent and said that the skipper wanted to see me.

"I understand you gave Lt. Sack some trouble last night?" he queried.
"Yes, Sir."

"I'll have to put you under house arrest for a couple of days."
"Yes, Sir."

House arrest in that place meant that he placed an armed guard at the door of the tent, and one couldn't leave except for meals and necessary privy stops. As I left his tent he stopped me, "Say Andy, the next time you do that be sure you take the rifle out from under his cot. That salt water raised hell with the firing mechanism."
"Yes, Sir."

Chapter 11
Entertainment

Our first taste of top entertainers began on the eve of our squadron's departure for overseas. A huge party was held and it so happened our "sponsor" was Bing Crosby. During the course of the evening, Bing and I happened to visit the restroom at the same time. I asked Bing if he would sing a tune with which I could harmonize and he obliged. I can't remember the tune but I do remember emerging from the men's room entertaining the gathering with our vocal rendition. Our offering drew huge cheers from that gathering of Marines.

We did have occasional USO shows at Makin. We saw Bob Hope and his troupe. It's true that he was tired and gave a lot of shows, but it was disappointing to see Bob dressed the same as we were. Lord knows we had seen enough of khakis. When Jack Benny came it was different. I'm sure he gave just as many shows as Hope, but he came out in a shiny blue suit, and Carole Lombard was in an evening dress that, to these eyes, was gorgeous. Couldn't help but appreciate that. Everybody in Jack's troupe looked stateside first class.

There were also movies that were seldom of interest to me. Normally, at night, we would resort to poker as a means of entertainment. The only comfortable place to play was the mess tent. First of all, it was the only place with lights, and secondly, the whole tent was netted, so mosquitoes were not quite so prevalent as in the smaller tents.

Two of us had purchased and brought with us a roulette wheel. We ran it and banked it for some time. Thankfully, we figured out before the players did that the wheel was crooked, that is to say, off balance. If one continually bet on the heavy side of the wheel, winning was a certainty. We did well until we suspected that others had learned the secret. We sold it to an army guy in their officers' club. Poker was again more dependable.

Chapter 12
Heroes & Jocks

Not too long after arriving at Makin we received word that a Navy pilot had been shot down at Wotje, and we were to be involved in a rescue attempt. It so happens that the pilot was a former All American running back, I think from Iowa. At the time, like everyone else, I knew his name well. When we arrived on scene, loaded up with bombs, he was probably a mile from shore in a raft that someone had dropped to him. There were fighters there also, and a couple of ships were off-shore pounding the beach with artillery. It was everyone's duty to shut down all of the shore batteries to provide cover for the rescue craft sent to pick him up. They did safely get him. I thought at the time that it was wonderful that there was no limit to the resources thrown into harm's way just to save one pilot. It didn't take too many days to find out that there were limits, but that in this case he was an All American. Good press!

Nothing has been said of the faithful gunner, hired to protect our hindside. What a job! I often thought of him, sitting there facing aft, not being able to see where we were going, rolling into a dive to go down backwards, facing the sky, wondering when we would pull out, and all of the time not being able to do a damned thing about it. Meanwhile, up front, on the other side of the wall of armor plate, the pilot was busy and, in my case, having a ball. The gunner, in my opinion, had a terrible job, and I was most fortunate in having one of the real good ones. Married with one kid, his nickname was "Pappy". He sat in a seat which was suspended in a ring of steel which would allow him to rotate 360 degrees. There were rudders, a throttle, and a stick fastened to the side of his quarters which could be thrust into a socket below, giving him the very basics of controls in case the pilot was hit. Also mounted on the ring supporting his seat was a pair of 30 caliber machine guns. That's why he was there! Fly facing aft, keep the eyes peeled for danger from anywhere in his line of sight and, via intercom, keep the pilot informed about what the other planes were doing, etc.

On many flights with no other planes, I had taught my gunner to make turns, climb, descend, and *(hopefully)* make some kind of a landing. He did have other skills, mainly radio and *(tongue in cheek)* radar. If he left his guns and faced forward, his cockpit also included the radio gear and a small radar screen.

Mounted on each wing was a small antenna which he could rotate, individually, from straight ahead to 90 degrees to the side. If the transmitted beam hit anything out there from which it would bounce back, the reward would be a blip on one side of a vertical line on the screen which was calibrated in miles. So, the gunner could proudly announce "Bogey at thirty miles to the left". By guiding the pilot and moving his antennas, the gunner could maneuver the plane into a position where the blip appeared on both sides of the screen when the target was dead ahead. This was radar in its infancy. The object creating the blip could be on the surface, an island perhaps, or maybe a whale. It could be in the air.. another plane maybe? In other words, at that stage of development radar was pretty much of a joke, but at times one could spot a ship with it. In fact, a ship generally showed up on his screen much better than an island. Primarily, though, he was a gunner, and hopefully whatever he may be called upon to fire at would not fall in line with either the rudder or the elevators of the plane in which he was a passenger.

The enlisted men were never allowed hard liquor, but they did have a noncoms' tent where the sergeants were allocated a bottle of beer now and then. Pappy deserved better, and I would sometimes reward him at the end of a flight with an exchange of canteens. There was a canteen mounted in the front cockpit which the line crew captain of each plane was to keep full of fresh water. In addition, each of us wore a belt while flying which supported a canteen, a pistol, and a huge knife. *(That must have been most uncomfortable for us.)* In this canteen on my belt I would often carry Seagrams VO. In that there was no ice on the island it was the only way to cool anything. Flying at 12000 feet for awhile seemed to cool it down a bit. At the end of some flights I'd suggest to Pappy that I'd swap him canteens if he had any water left.

"Yes, sir" he answered. He always called me "Sir". Never was anything else said about the exchange, but I noticed at the conclusion of any flight which carried us up into altitude, that he was somewhat reluctant to leave in case I had anything else to say.

Never, except once, did I ever take a nip from that canteen on the belt.

The mechanics had made a mechanical improvement on the bombing release mechanism of the planes. We had always had a simple bomb release handle on the left side of the cockpit sort of forward and below the other controls. When about ready to release, one would move the left hand from the throttle to the bomb release handle and at the proper moment give a jerk. The improvement installed was a button on the throttle, which would allow release without taking one's hand from the throttle.

Habit, however, is a most compelling dictator. At the appropriate moment, my hand moved from the throttle to the release handle, a jerk, back to the throttle, and then pull out. No bomb release. Well, the SBD wasn't really designed to pull out of dive with the 1000 pound bomb still attached, and there were some palm trees definitely in peril before I was forced to admit another pilot error.

The other planes were making a rendezvous above, wondering if I had been shot. I called, asked them to wait a moment, that I wanted to make another run. This time from just about 6000 feet, I dove and steeled myself to the discipline of pushing that damned button on the throttle and got rid of the bomb. After seeing that I was OK, the rest headed for home. That left Pappy and me alone to enjoy a leisurely ride back without having to worry about anyone else.

With no other responsibilities, why not check out that VO on the way home? There was no wind *(very unlike any other day)*, the sea was a dead calm, and the wind sock hung loosely from its tower by the runway. There was a pointer next to the runway indicating the direction of take-offs or landings, and it was pointed in the other direction but I hadn't looked at it. All other planes had landed, so there was no traffic pattern to observe. Either direction, then, would be OK for landing. As I made my approach, I later learned that they were firing red flares and red lights from the control tower, but curiously I never saw them. For some reason I "landed" about ten feet above the level of the runway, and upon contact blew the left tire. *(They don't make them like they used to.)*

Like most wheeled vehicles, an SBD is hard to steer if one wheel doesn't roll, so we headed for the lagoon on the left. This seemed to bring out the best in me and just before the watery entry I unlocked the tail wheel and ground-looped to bring the thing to a stop. I looked out to the other side and there stood Pappy.

"How did you get out so fast?" I hollered.

"I wasn't going to go in the drink with you", he countered.

I didn't have time to upbraid him for insubordination because our flight surgeon appeared on the wing. He, of course, thought I had been shot and had made some kind of heroic effort in saving the lives of the pilot and gunner. One look at my eyes and he said, "Jump in the jeep, Andy, and let's get out of here." I never took a nip in an airplane again, but did have the mechanics remove that methods-improvement throttle device. That tire was the only piece of equipment that I ever damaged while in the service.

In paying some tribute to Pappy, it must be said that in addition to being always very respectful and polite he was also very observant and kept me informed always about the location and condition of the other planes, especially our two wingmen.

Chapter 13
Jaluit

Jaluit, of our four target neighbors, was by far the best protected, best developed, and well armed of the group of islands. It was always with a feeling of relief that we counted heads after a strike and headed for home.

On one of our earlier missions there, the targets for the day were their big guns. It always seemed to me that in a dive, the advantage had to go to the plane. In fact, I always pitied those poor bastards on the ground, tilted way over on their backs, firing straight up, and all they had to shoot at was a nose of a plane which wouldn't stand still, but which kept circling around as it grew ever closer. Truth is, we seldom got hit while in a dive. However, the smart ground gunners knew that when one pulled out of a dive the wings had to be level, so if he could anticipate the pull-out time all he had to do was hold straight in front of the nose, set up a stream and let the plane fly through it.

On this day we encountered just such an enlightened soul, and whether he was firing a 20 or a 40 mm rapid fire I don't know. However, at pull-out, one hit us just behind the gas tank in the right wing just about a foot from the fuselage. It sent a terrifying shock wave through the air-frame, and each of us looked out to see a gaping hole large enough to put one's head through, helmet and all. I was checking the controls to see if we could still fly this thing when Pappy's voice calmly sounded over the intercom, "Sir...I think we've been hit." The sound of one's own laughter in such a situation sure breaks the tension. My only chuckling response was, "My God, Pappy, but you're perceptive."

I don't know what ever happened to the pictures the squadron photographer took of each of us with our heads, *(one at a time)* sticking up through that hole. Hopefully, Pappy has his. The photographer, like the intelligence officer, didn't like me very well.

46

Time was a constant enemy when we were not in the air. We played a little softball, some read, a couple of us kicked the football around. Non-existent on the island was a really good chair for resting and during this slack period it occurred to me to create one. When finished, I was the proud owner of an original, comfortable rocking chair with palm fronds for rockers, wide arm rests, a retractable foot rest and a writing table that swiveled up from the side to the arm rests. Simultaneously a stationary shelf also came up on the writer's left side. To complete the comfort atmosphere, a cigarette vending apparatus was attached to the right arm. Whenever the nicotine habit dictated, the occupant of the chair merely pressed a pressure point and voila, a cigarette miraculously emerged. When we left, Pinaduke, the king of the tribe of natives on the island, claimed the chair as his own. It thus assumed its rightful place as a king's throne.

Always time for comfort

Wind propelled laundry machine 8' diameter propellor

Makin barber - King

"Redistribution of wealth"

During this period it was necessary to eat, and in anticipation of this many of the guys had filled their foot lockers with spam and other non-perishable snack foods before we left Eva. It proved to be good planning, because the fare served up at the mess tent really got pretty bad. I remember the color more than the taste. Green comes to mind for whatever was served, and that includes the meat, whenever available. Horse meat is about the only meat we ever had that I can recall. For me it wasn't too bad, but some of the guys couldn't eat it.

We observed that the natives, when the tide was just right, would go out to the reef at night with burning torches soaked in some kind of oil, form a line parallel to the reef, and then slowly head for the shore. As they waved their fire-brands the fish would run in front of them and the natives would actually drive them right up on shore. There others waited, would catch the assortment of fish with their hands, and take off.

We, being hungry and well equipped, improved on the process and used our Coleman lanterns for the above exercise. Our guys on shore would have a fire of gasoline and oil under garbage cans full of boiling water. After cleaning, we would throw all of these things into the boiling water and have a feast. The feast also included lobsters which would scurry along the bottom ahead of the light. By the time we left the island, most of the guys had traded their Coleman lanterns for some trinkets of the natives. The natives were fishing with Colemans and our guys were fishing with torches. I never traded so have no trinkets.

Every once in a while for food and entertainment we were treated to a rare evening. A merchant vessel tied up overnight proved to be a most inviting target. They, of course, had no booze on board, and we, of course, had very lousy food. A couple of us would make it a point to get aboard, meet up with their officers, and arrange a special evening. At night we would board with a case of beer and a couple bottles of VO. They would respond by cooking steaks, yes, honest-to-God steaks, with frozen vegetables, baked potatoes, and even butter. One such night it was an English vessel, and the evening was uproarious. Their stories and accents were delightful. I'll never forget one of their songs, the verses of which cannot be repeated here, but the chorus went:

"I don't want to be a soldier,
I don't want to go to war,
I'd rather hang around Picadilly on the ground
Living off the earnings of a high-born lay-dee.
Call out the army and the old brigade,
They'll set England free,
Call out your mother, your sister, and your brother,
But for Cris' sake, DON'T CALL ME!"

When sung with the appropriate accent and the proper verses, it was hilarious. There were more, but the memory doesn't allow for more than one. What a great respite from the doldrums of the day.

The morning and evening search flights to our neighbors proved to be, for me, the most enjoyable. We would set off in pairs, each assigned two of the four islands. Upon approach, we would normally split up, and each would circle the atoll in opposite directions, get back together, head for the other assigned island, and do it again. Each would, then, do his own thing while searching for signs of ships or subs in the area. However, it was a war, and some of us felt anything below was fair game. The odds were not very good, but it was exhilarating to find some stationary or moving targets and try out those twin fifties, or maybe even a depth charge. We always carried depth charges instead of bombs on these search missions as our primary target most likely would be a sub.

On one such flight to Mille, we were circling on the lagoon side of the atoll at about 500 feet, when, much to my surprise we spotted a ship. It was well camouflaged, nestled in sort of a cove, and tucked under palm branches and netting very close to shore. It was obviously a supply vessel with a very low profile, not very large, maybe 200 feet in length. Was it here to supply those here, take some of them out, maybe both? How long had it been here? I'd never seen it before. All was quiet. Apparently they didn't want to give away its position if we didn't see it.

How do you make an SBD look nonchalant? We slowly angled away as if going to cross the atoll and leave, gradually gaining altitude all the time. We couldn't get high enough to make a dive, because it couldn't be seen from above. Some altitude was necessary, however, in order to get enough speed to at least jump over the coral strip and land on the ocean side if shot down. A few thousand feet was enough, and we slowly turned back. Yes, it was still there, and all was still quiet. Our course casually took us in the direction of the target, hoping we wouldn't alert anyone to our intentions.

At about the time we nosed over to get serious, all hell broke loose. It was a ship, and it was well defended all right. Tracers and staccato flashes, coming from both sides of that thing suggested that our presence was not welcome. If lucky, I could "toss" the depth charge in there, and hopefully get it close enough to do some damage. Then, skip over the trees, out on the ocean side and be on our way. That's the way it worked. We saw the explosion but couldn't see whether or not we were successful in doing any damage because now we were on the ocean side and could not see back through the trees.

Again, back at Makin, I had to report to that cadet reject what we had seen and what we had done. He pooh-poohed the story naturally, so I made a suggestion. "Grab your camera, Sack, and we'll run back and have a look at it right now." "Looking" at anything which might have a gun around it was not on Sack's list of things to do, let alone "look at it" with me.

"No way," was his only response. I then suggested that he send a photography plane in there and take a picture to see if it got away, and if it did, we should go looking for it. I could identify on a map exactly where we had spotted it.

The next day, after looking over the pictures, he informed me that there was an "old" hulk laying on its side in there. He concluded that it had probably been there all the time and we had never seen it. Remembering the sleeping cot incident, I let it go. I'm sure he reported to the higher ups that our squadron had spotted and sunk a supply ship that had been carefully camouflaged in the lagoon at Mille.

There was a program initiated for the R&R *(Rest & Relaxation)* of Marine pilots which was fantastic. In theory a guy was to get one week at THE rest home in Honolulu after every twenty five missions. Of course, nobody got there that often, but I did get to go there twice. The "Home" was a millionaire's mansion on Waikiki just down from the Royal Hawaiian Hotel. The owner had donated it to the Marines for just such a purpose. It was managed by a "Housemother" whose black book was unbelievable. There was only room for eight or ten of us at a time and each morning we were greeted by "Mom" asking if anyone wanted a girl friend for the day. The girls in her black book were not the kind that many of the guys had in mind. Those could be found in Honolulu, I guess, but hers were really nice, classy gals who were afraid of being caught on the street in the city, but enjoyed having a date with a gentleman now and then.

We were "gentlemen", you know, by act of Congress. "Mom" would ask what talents we preferred, one at a time that is. One might want to play golf, another tennis, maybe hiking or whatever. She had just the one in her book. I asked one day for a girl that liked to play bridge, and was rewarded by a black haired beauty who could have matched up with Charles Goren. A sailor headed out about ten in the morning in a big station wagon to pick up the requested girls. Upon his return, introductions were made and the pairings began for the day. In the afternoon at four o'clock, the girls were to be there ready to be delivered home. There were no girls allowed in the home after about four in the afternoon.

The service at the home was unlike anything I'd ever experienced. There was a Filipino tending the bar, which was open 24 hours a day, and a chef in the kitchen serving real red meat, vegetables, milk, butter, etc. upon request, and again 24 hours a day. We lucked out by having a pilot from some squadron *(only about two from any one squadron were there at a time)* who could really play the piano. So, late into the night we sang songs, listened to his composing, were served drinks, and above all, ate sandwich after sandwich until collapse time came. All of this time while we were gaining weight we were also being paid. Incredible!

It should be said here that never was a diary kept, so these stories are in no particular sequence, nor could I properly assign a sequence if called upon to do so. Sometime during the stay at Makin, the higher-ups made a decision which was based upon some of the antics of the combatants. A very good decision one might agree, to break up some of these squadrons. The guys had been together too long! At the time there was also a dive-bombing squadron based on Majuro and we merged with them. How the skippers decided who would go and who would stay remains a mystery, but apparently the idea was to break up all tent-mates. Luckily my gear didn't have to be moved, so as 14 or 20 arrived from Majuro looking for a place to sleep, I invited the one who looked most disapproving of all of this to bunk with me. He acknowledged with only a grunt. A few days later he even told me his name. He was an excellent choice and in defiance of the skipper's advice became a very good friend. Sam Larue and I remained friends until his early death from Alzheimers.

In all fairness to Sack, I complimented him one day for accurately identifying and locating the girlie houses on Jaluit. That was the only island where we had properly located where the girls were housed and in this instance they were actually there. They were located toward the edge of the cluster of buildings on the island and we never touched them. In fact some of our guys made a point of driving by after every run just to wave at the girls who might be outside hanging clothes on a line or just standing around watching the goings on. They came to know that we would leave them alone and they would always wave back.

Just in the last couple of years the Japanese government has admitted to forcing women to service the men in the armed forces during WWII and has made some kind of payment to those still alive. I'm sure those payments don't include the natives who were forced into slavery as the Japanese did their island hopping.

Wotje and Maloelap left no particular memories except for the rescue of the All American. We made regular bombing runs on them and twice a day visits, but we either destroyed most of their ammunition, or they were saving it for an anticipated invasion on our part. After the first few months, in my recollection, there were very few shots fired when we went in to look around or even when we had scheduled bombing runs on identifiable targets. No so at Jaluit or Mille.

Jaluit was the most challenging for the twice a day check ups. One could usually find some worthwhile targets if paying attention. We found a little operating steam engine one day on their little railroad. The crew members scurried from tree to tree as Pappy and I dismembered the little engine. Pappy had little opportunity to practice gunnery unless we worked at it but by laying the plane over on its side while circling the target one would put the gunner in a good position to fire. Other targets there included small boats of many kinds and it was fun to catch them out in the Lagoon racing to shore. These forays did not go undetected and some patch jobs were required as a result of such encounters.

Perhaps the personnel loss that most affected me for the entire tour occurred just before heading back to the states. The job was done here. All four islands were well neutralized, and it was time for our squadron to move on closer to Japan. We were being replaced by new pilots a few at a time. Our married boys were relieved first and those of us who remained trained the replacements in whatever the assignments were.

One afternoon I met a young *(I guess we were all young)* pilot who was to go with me for the evening check at Jaluit. He informed me that he was newly married, his wife was pregnant and that he didn't want to be a hero. All he wanted to do was survive and get back home. I had always felt sorry for the few married men we had in our squadron. Their attitude was much different from those of us who were single and here was a lad who exemplified that "Let's get out of here" mind set. They really didn't belong. At any rate, I agreed. I told him that normally we'd head down to see what we could find, but that in this case we'd do only what we had to do, that is to circle the place to see if there were any surface vessels or subs to be found. I assured him that we'd stay at pretty good altitude where they wouldn't waste ammunition shooting at us.

As we approached the island I motioned him back off a couple of plane lengths so he could relax and see the island rather than keep his eyes on me. We climbed up to about 2000 feet and gradually turned to make a circle of the atoll, and I noticed a shore battery was firing, apparently at us. That's stupid, I thought, we're out of range. We had to be about a mile from shore. My thoughts were interrupted by Pappy calling, "He's been hit!" I turned around, and sure enough, he was on fire. His gunner went out first, and the pilot followed. Both chutes opened OK, and we followed them down. Somehow Pappy managed to get the life raft out of our plane and drop it to them, and both were able to get in, so apparently had not been injured.

Majuro had a few PBYs, a large twin engine seaplane for search and rescue work. We had immediately called the base at Majuro and called for help. One PBY arrived about an hour and a half later with darkness approaching and found some unusually heavy seas. The wind, unfortunately, was carrying the raft directly toward the island. When the PBY began circling the shore batteries opened up, so Pappy and I were busy trying to shut them down. After a couple of passes, the pilot of the PBY came on the air and announced that he couldn't land. If he did manage to get it down, there was no way he could get it back off of the water. I know he was right, but the destroyer on the way wouldn't get there until well after dark, and he couldn't very well do anything until morning. In a couple of hours the raft would be ashore. Their fate was sealed. Low on gas, and with dark closing in, we flew slowly by and waved goodbye. All the brass wanted to see us and ordered that we fly to Majuro instead of Makin. That was a long, long flight. Not in miles, but in time for recollection. Why did he get it instead of me? Just a poor Japanese gunner I guess, he didn't give me enough lead. Why, when we were being so careful, when he'd never even fired a shot, would a young guy with a pregnant wife waiting for his return be so unlucky? They had had plenty of chances to get me for a year and a half, but no, they unfortunately hit this young chap.

The Marine Colonel and the Navy Captain raised all kinds of hell, but I didn't really hear much of what they had to say. I kept wondering what it was I would tell his wife. Not many weeks later, after more pilots arrived to relieve us, I was able to find out. After getting his name and address, the first thing I did after returning to the states was to call her. Some consolation! I don't remember much about what I told her, but do remember telling her that he had not been hit, that he was alive and well and would be picked up by the Japs, where he would be well cared for as would any prisoner of war. All the time while saying this I kept thinking of that poor devil staked out on the runway at Mille, dead or alive. She didn't respond, just continued sobbing, and tried a blubbering, "Thanks for calling."

Chapter 14
Back to the States

I was off to Denver then for a couple of weeks of R & R. Mom used to ask why it was that I didn't have any ribbons, when all of the other servicemen seemed to have so many. The reason was that the Army had trivialized the medals to a point where they really had no meaning. An Air Medal, by Army standards, was awarded for every five missions, and a Distinguished Flying Cross after every twenty five. A quick calculation determined that I could, by those standards, have about 18 Air Medals and three DFCs. That's a big load to carry. Truth is, I didn't even have one of anything, other than theater ribbons, so for most Marine pilots the wings would have to suffice. Some months after discharge, I received a call from the Marine Corps telling me I had been awarded the Air Medal, and would I like to receive it at a full dress parade at Lowry Field *(An Army base in Denver)*, or should they just mail it to my home address. After receiving it in the mail, we did keep it for some years, and the last I saw of it, young son Nels had hung it on a post in the blueberry patch in Enumclaw.

After a couple of weeks leave at home it was off to the new assignment. One of the good guys in our squadron had been assigned to instrument school in Atlanta. I talked to Mac about a sister of mine who was stationed there, whom I hadn't seen for a couple of years. Please look her up for me, I asked, and say "Hello." Being one of the good guys and very dependable, he did as he was asked. A couple of months later he called and asked if it was OK with me if he married her. So, one of the really good guys became a brother-in-law. Meanwhile, Sam headed off for someplace in Florida for another dive-bombing outfit, and for me it was off to Cherry Point, NC where they were putting a squadron together for the invasion of Japan.

Major Mac was the skipper, a big guy who had played football at USC and who was an excellent pilot. Our planes were SB2Cs, a bigger and better dive bomber made by Curtis. There was a problem here. Anything made by Curtis reminded me of the thing we flew to Midway. This was somewhat the same. It had 2000 hp, was naturally a little faster and could carry more weight, but as big as it was it was underpowered too. In a dive it was no match for the SBD. It was big, a lot of work to fly, and a poor substitute for its predecessor. No matter! Equipment upgrading was necessary. There were just a few of us who had been in combat, so we were placed as division leaders. The others had been instructors, or had just graduated, so we were to be their instructors now.

There was to be a demonstration for some of the senators and Pentagon brass of Marine ground forces in action, supported by Marine air. This was held someplace close to Washington, D.C. We were to be a part of that demonstration. Major Mac had to go up there to spend the day with the brass observing and explaining his squadron's part in the action, so the squadron was led by executive officer. A great, tall viewing stand had been built for the observers, probably a couple of hundred yards from the goings-on. When we arrived, the "grunts" on the ground were attacking a fortified pill-box, and it was our job to wipe it out.

To fully understand this story, one must know something about ordnance. Every bomb has to have a detonator and in our case a windmill propeller. A wire through the propeller prevented it from turning and becoming an "active" bomb until the pilot was ready to dive, at which time he pulled the wire. So, as the bomb fell the propeller turned, thus arming the bomb and preventing the dropping of a "dud".

The day of the demonstration was a terrible day for bombing. The wind was blowing hard in different directions, and our guys were hitting everything BUT the pill-box and the reviewing stand. It must have been embarrassing for Major Mac. Ours was the last division. I held up my hand and grabbed my wrist so all of these youngsters would remember to "arm" their bombs. Then over the wingman to the left and down on the bunker. It was a rough ride down, but even so I was quite sure that we hit it OK. Then as we pulled out, "Didn't see where it hit, Sir" said the gunner.

That night at the officers' club at Cherry Point, Major Mac was waiting for me at the bar.

"Great job, Andy," he says.

"The only time in my life I ever forgot to arm a bomb," was my meek reply.

"You know," he went on, "I told those fellows on the stand to keep their eyes on the leader of that last division. He'll get the bunker for you."

He then turned to face me and look me right in the eye as he went on. "I was right. We all watched the bomb hit dead center on that pill-box. No explosion, not even a wisp of smoke!"

He continued, "I covered for you. I told them that we got a bomb now and then that was a dud."

Thus ended the illustrious career of a once proud Marine pilot.

A few days later, the ready room was abuzz with the news that we had dropped an atomic bomb on Hiroshima. Our group was about ready to embark for who knew where en route to Japan. "Major Mac," I implored, "let me out of here. If there's a war on, there's no way I want to miss it. But please don't let me go over there to be a policeman." Mac complied, and shortly thereafter I went to be what I thought was discharged. That's when I learned the true meaning of the expression, "Once a Marine, always a Marine". So, "inactive" Robert E Anderson headed back to the challenges of schooling, to be greeted by professors who were mad because we had expended so much energy in our war with Japan, and viewed by students as "Old Squares," somehow out of place.

The experiences narrated above were crammed into a short, but exciting four year period of my life. Perhaps one should not refer to a war as an enjoyable experience, as Lord knows it certainly wasn't for those who slugged it out on the ground. For me, however, it was a most enjoyable experience. Imagine getting to do all of those things, being able to use all of the latest expensive toys, and actually be paid for it. Pay, I think, amounted to sixty nine dollars a month when enlisted, and bumped up to about $225 a month when commissioned. We did receive flight pay above that which was a lot…50% above base pay. In retrospect, to have had military discipline during the formative years of my early twenties was a great foundation for the rest of my life.

Truth is, it was a great privilege to be able to serve, and for me it was the most exciting period of my life. Interesting, also, to have served in all three branches. Two years in college in the Army ROTC horse-drawn Field Artillery, then as a cadet we were in the Navy as Seamen 2nd class, commissioned then in the Marine Corps. Although the cache of collar bars was never uncovered, most of us were promoted to First Lieutenant status after being overseas for a few months, and for me, at least, that's where I remained for the balance of active years. After the time of change to inactive status I received a letter informing me of promotion to Captain.

I've been told that nine of our squadron pilots were called back into service for the Korean conflict, and that of the nine, eight were killed by infantry rifle fire. Apparently the Lord had his hand on me in avoiding that call, just as he had cared for me the prior four years. ***To Him I shall always be grateful.***

A Short History of the SBD Dive Bombers

Scout Bomber Douglas, a.k.a. slow but deadly

While the design of the SBD Dauntless might have seemed a bit cumbersome, the aircraft proved resilient in the face of adversity. Developed by Norththrop, the SBD was eventually absorbed and refined by Douglas. Powered by a single row Wright-R-1820 series engine rated at 850 horsepower, the SBD-1 could achieve a top speed of 250 mph, a ceiling of over 25,000 feet, and a range of well over 1,000 miles. Subsequent models performed even better, with the final version SBD-6 boasting a 1350 horsepower engine. Meanwhile, Japanese fighters had more agility and firepower, but were very lightly armored.

Although the SBD had a slow start at the beginning of the war, it more than proved itself at the Battle of the Coral Sea. Then in June of 1942 at the Battle of Midway, SBDs sank all four of the Japanese carriers thus reversing the balance of sea power in the Pacific. Serving primarily off American carriers, the Dauntless would go down in history as a legend, not only as an exceptional aircraft but also for the bravery of her crews.

SBDs had a reputation for being able to absorb heavy battle damage, which was a great asset to the 20 Marine squadrons that flew them until the end of the war. Possessing a very low loss ratio, the aircraft was credited with the destruction of hundreds of enemy planes, 26 large ships including carriers, cruisers and destroyers along with a host of smaller boats.

The first flight of the SBD-1 was made on May 1, 1940. Continually improved, nearly 6000 SBDs were produced through 1944.

Photo courtesy of www.historylink101.com
Information derived from www.boeing.com; militaryfactory.com & aviation-history.com.

The Dauntless

"The Dauntless had established an enviable record for reliability and toughness, and its career in the Pacific had certainly been illustrious. Yet, from the performance standpoint it had been a very mediocre aeroplane, and having operated for much of the time in a non air superiority environment, one is left with a very deep respect for its crews. I personally did not find the hidden quality in the Dauntless that I had sought on the strength of its remarkable operational reputation. I could only conclude that it was to be numbered among that handful of aeroplanes that have achieved outstanding success against all odds."

Lt Cdr Eric "Winkle' Brown, RAE Farnborough, 1944

MOUSIEVILLE
HOME OF
THE FAMOUS
"RED MOUSIES"
of
VMSB-245.
HERE ROOST THE WORLD'S BEST
DIVE BOMBERS

A Day's Work

September 1944
Awaiting green light for take-off

Ground Crew

"It takes more than one to keep it flying. One to fly and three to keep it in the air."

Up top: Andy
Left to right: Steve, Barnes & Gaither

Rendezvous - Makin July 1944

Here we Come - Relaxed!

After continued laboring for altitude, the target, Mille, was in sight, and we had about 12,000 feet to squander to get to the target for the day. The target was a piece of cake, just dismantle the runways. Funny, the sky now had a bunch of small black clouds at about our altitude which hadn't been there before. We nosed over a little to pick up some speed between here and where we'd roll over into a dive. Also, we did engage in some evasive tactics, still being careful to be very smooth in deference to those wingmen. Arm the bombs, roll over into a dive, and now one could see where those black clouds were coming from. Bright flashes from gun emplacements all over the island gave away the positions of their big guns, then as one got lower, the different staccato flashes of 40 millimeter and 20 mm rapid fire machine guns replaced the large flashes of the 90 millimeter guns which had greeted our arrival. These smaller weapons though also with explosive heads, left some streams of tracers. Rather pretty. Fourth of July kind of thing!

Look Out Below!

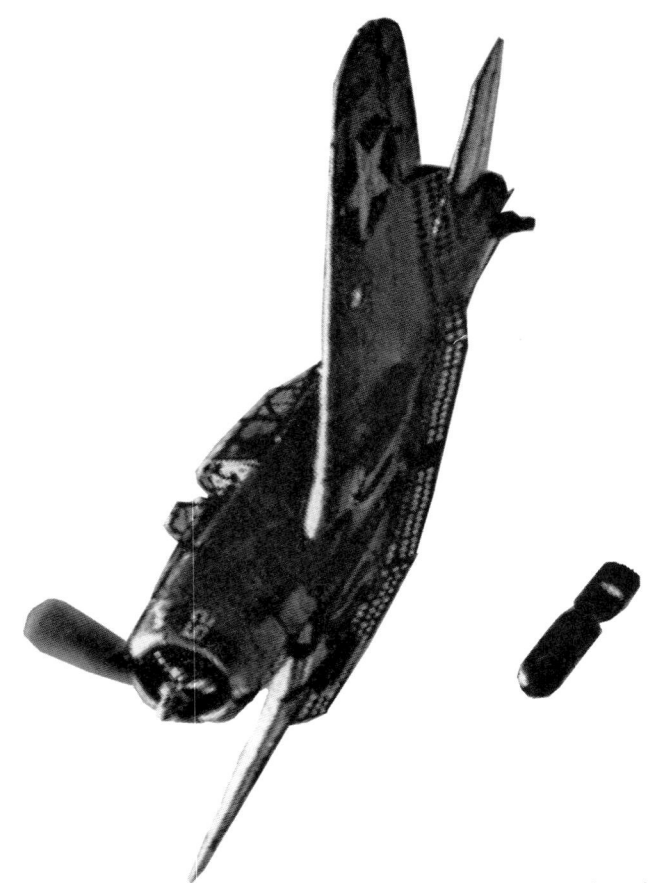

A U.S. Navy Douglas SBD Dauntless releasing a bomb
Note the extended trailing edge dive brakes

Then, keep one eye on the altimeter, the large hand rapidly unwinding, and as it passes 1000 feet pull the release, get out of the dive, head for the water, cross controls, and skid from one side to the other, hoping the gunners on the ground will take the bait and lead you in the direction the plane appears to be traveling. Hopefully, by the time he gets it figured out you'll be out of range. Careful, also, not to get too close to the water; some of the larger shells put up quite a water wall which one wouldn't want to fly through.

Heading Home

Breaking up for landing

WWII MEMOIRS

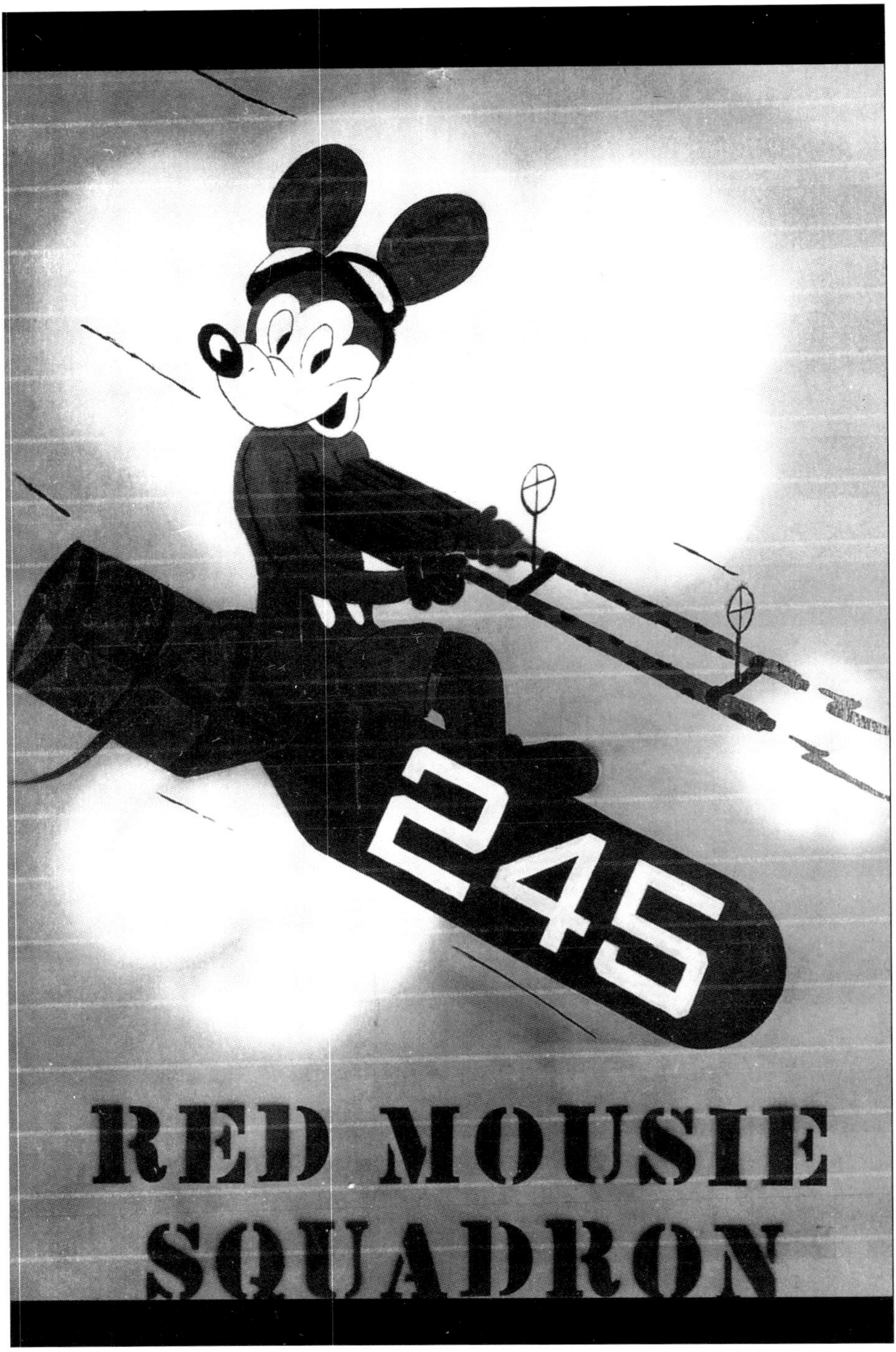
245
RED MOUSIE
SQUADRON

67

Sitting: LaRue, Hastings, Baxter, Curtiss, Grube, Bailly, Hartmann, Oster, Sire, Daniel, Watkins, Barber

Standing: Vincent, Booher, Sannebeck, Baker, Arledge, Rollins, Mitchell, Patterson - Maj., Halladay - Maj., Sackett, Monaghan, McGarr, Steele, Archbold, Atkinson

Sitting on wings: Harrower, Sparks, Jackson, Ross, Kerr, Paine, Cooper, Dean, Fillingim, Verhime, McClelland, Lemmons, Anderson, Bowers, Deal, Norvell

Standing on wings: Robinson, Perrin

Note: All names listed from left to right
Taken December 8, 1944 Eva Marine Airfield, Oahu

Missing: Perrin - Pilot, Mahaffey - Pilot, Dallmeyer - Pilot, Daily - Ground Officer Engineering, Fillingim - Ground Officer Material, Oster - Ground Officer Defense

Taken February 7, 1944 Midway Island

Back row: DEAL, MURPHY, SMITH, STANARD, VINCENT, ENRIGHT, ROTH, GREELY, JONES, TRAYNOR

Front row: HALL, MITCHELL, McEVOY, WEIL, TURNER, COOPER, BOOHER, KING, WRIGHT, ROBINSON, PAINE, NORVELL, SCOTT, ABBLIT

Ground Officers in picture: Watkins - Mess Officer, Deal - Aerial Gunner, Vincent - Doctor, M.D., Enright - Adjutant & Gunnery, Weil - Transportation & Communication, Wright - not a member of VMSB 245, Scott - Ordnance

Visiting an Old Friend!
2010

Of the 5,936 SBDs built from 1940 tp 1944 when production ceased, there are 15 remaining:

10 on display

4 under restoration

1 airworthy

Bob visiting an old friend

73

WWII MEMOIRS

Author's Biography

Robert *(Andy)* Anderson was born in 1922, in Denver Colorado, just the right age for the "big one". He was the fifth child of Esther and Eno Anderson, the only boy with five sisters. His love of flying started early. He remembers riding his bicycle out to a nearby airport where he hung around, fascinated with the planes. At the age of 12, a sympathetic WWI pilot gave him his first flight in a WWI Spad.

He graduated from East High in 1940 at age 17, attended Colorado Aggies *(now CSU)* where he joined the ROTC Program. Forty hours in a CPT flying course earned him his pilot's license. After two years of college he was eligible for officer training where the Navy and then the Marine Corps trained him as a dive bomber pilot. His love of flying never wavered and, contrary to many who served in the military, WWII provided him with many positive memories.

After serving in the Pacific, he was placed on inactive status and returned to college where he graduated with a degree in Civil Engineering. In a real life "love at first sight" meeting in a cafe up Big Thompson, he proposed to and soon after married the cook, waitress and sole proprietor, Shirley Denter. Thereafter, his flying adventures were in a rented plane with his wife and three children, visiting colleges, friends and relatives.

Currently he resides in Kalispell, Montana with Shirley, his wife of 63 years, and Duffy, a Welsh Terrier and his constant shadow. Briefly he owned a small aircraft and enjoyed flying Montana skies before acknowledging plane ownership was just too expensive. Still the sound of a flyover of a locally owned F4U brings him to his feet.

Andy and Jib, 1945

Andy and Duffy, 2011

Parents' Biography

Bob was raised in a conservative household; parents Esther and Eno Anderson were Swedish Lutherans. Esther, a product of the time and the culture, made the home a place of constancy and contentment. As the only boy, Bob looked to his Dad for guidelines to living. At age 18 Eno emigrated to the U.S. at the turn of the century. He developed a strong work ethic, remembering shoveling coal in a wheelbarrow to be pushed up a ramp and dumped...all for a nickel a ton. He strongly supported college educations for each child, not only for his son but also for his five daughters so they could achieve success in their chosen field. As an adult, Bob realized his father never showed signs of stress or overwork, even during the Depression when concern for his family and business had to weigh heavily on his mind. Knowing Eno, one would realize his unwavering faith in God carried him through those times.

Perhaps his father's greatest influence was his appreciation and loyalty for his adopted country. However, he retained a love of Swedish culture and once monthly their home resonated with the sound of Swedish being spoken as Eno played poker with his Swedish cronies while the wives prepared Swedish food. Yes, Lutefisk! Otherwise, only English was spoken in the home. Eno believed strongly that learning the language of your adopted country was a vital part of assimilation. His loyalty to the U.S. was tested when Bob announced his intention of joining the Marines. Both parents deplored the thought of their only son going to war, but supported him in his volunteering for the Marine Corps.

Andy's Dad Eno, 1981

Dad, Andy and Mom

Mom and Andy

Eno and Esther Anderson

Home Base: Map of Makin Island

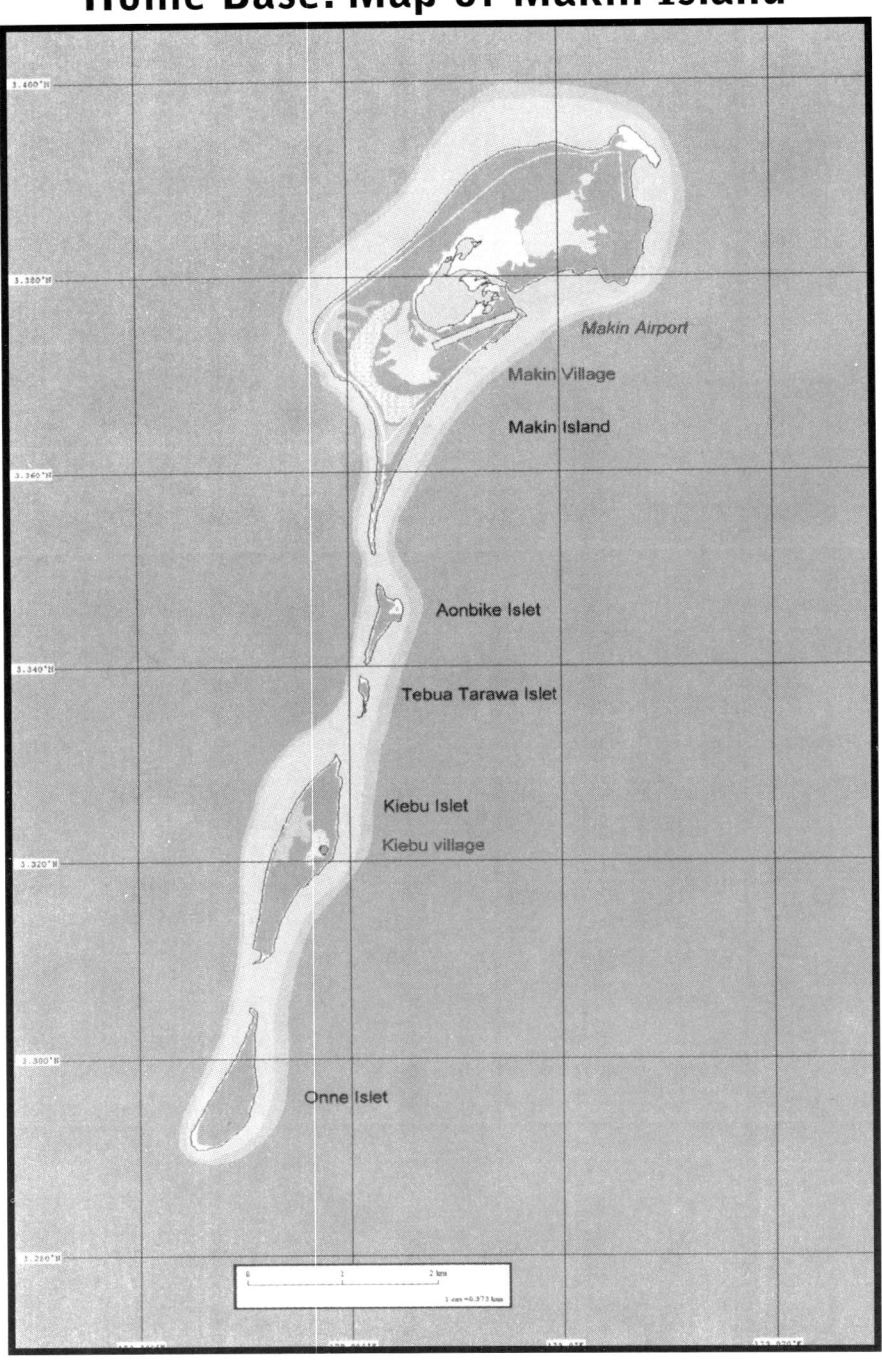

"When once you have tasted flight, you will forever walk the earth with your eyes turned skyward, for there you have been, and there you will always long to return."

Leonardo da Vinci, 16th century artist, expert in other fields of knowledge including aerodynamics

Notes